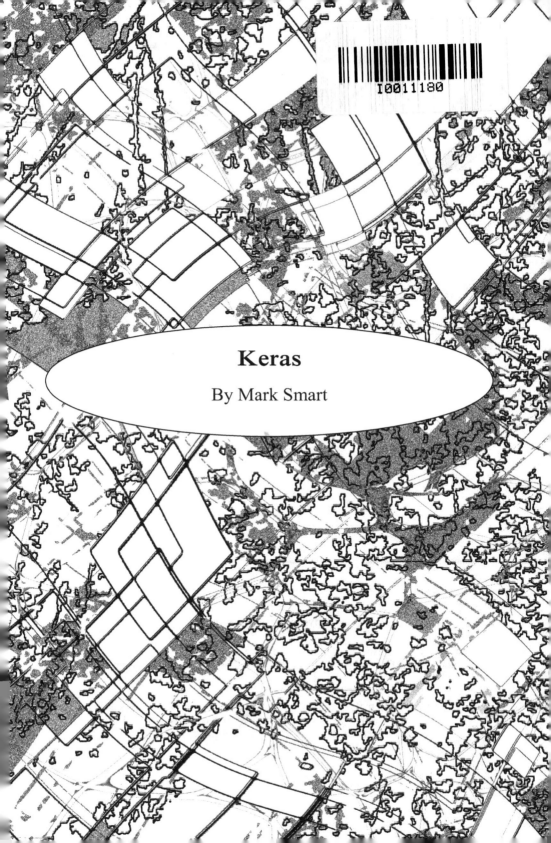

# Keras

By Mark Smart

**Keywords**: python, keras python, scikit learn, deeplearning4j, tensorflow keras, keras deep learning, numpy python, python programming, theano, keras tensorflow, deep learning with keras, cntk, python tensorflow, lambda.

## Reader Feedback

Feedbacks from my readers are always welcome, it's important to me and your review will help other readers.

Please let me know what you think. Send me general feedback; e-mail: **gloria.kemer@gmail.com** and mention please the book title in the subject of your message.

# What this book covers:

Preface                                               7
What is Keras model?                                  8
Basic Classification Tasks with Keras               72
Keras for Image Classification                      81
Keras for Text Classification                       85
Advanced Keras                                      91
Final notes                                        101

# Preface

The use of neural networks for data processing has been on the rise. Neural network models are good for extraction of patterns, trends and relationships between the various variables in a dataset. The good thing with neural network models is that they are the best for processing huge datasets which may be difficult to process using other machine learning models. Keras is a machine learning library good for development of neural networks. It comes with numerous features that make it easy for its users to create neural network models from scratch. This book guides you on how to use the Keras library to build your own neural network models for data process.

Enjoy reading!

# 1

## What is Keras model?

Keras is written in Python for deep learning library. It is used for development of neural networks and it can run on top libraries such as Theano, TensorFlow and CNTK. During its development, it was meant for fast experimentation. The library was developed for human beings rather than machines, which has made it more user-friendly. It gives a high priority to user experience. The user is only expected to go through a few steps before completing any particular action. Keras can also be extended with much ease. It is easy for us to add to it new modules and the existing modules comes with many examples. The ability of Keras to allow the creation of new modules for expressiveness has made it a good library for advanced research.

### Keras Layers

All the Keras layers have some common methods. Examples of these methods include the following:

- layer.get_weights() - this method returns the weights of a layer in the form of a list of Numpy arrays.
- layer.set_weights(weights) - this method sets the weights of a layer obtained from a list of Numpy arrays. The arrays must have the same shape as those obtained from the above method.
- layer.get_config() - this method returns a dictionary with a configuration of a layer.

There are several layers in Keras library. Let us discuss them:

### Core Layers

Keras has many core layers. Let us discuss them:

### Masking

The masking layer works by setting the output values to 0 when an entire last dimension of an input is equal to *mask_value*, with the default value being a 0.

The layer expects an input tensor of 3 dimensions with the shape samples, timesteps, and features. Let us make some imports sand create some debug functions that we will need for this section of core layers:

**from keras.layers.core import \***

**from keras import backend as K**

**def call_f(inp, method, input_data):**

  **f = K.function([inp], [method])**

  **return f([input_data])[0]**

**def print_out(layer, input_data, train=True):**

  **if hasattr(layer, 'previous'):**

    **print call_f(layer.previous.input, layer.get_output(train=train), input_data)**

  **else:**

    **print call_f(layer.input, layer.get_output(train=train), input_data)**

We can now call a Masking layer with 3D tensor and pass two rows of data to it:

**print_out(Masking(mask_value=1), [[[1, 1, 0], [1, 1, 1]]])**

The last rows will get masked as it's the row having the whole content match a mask_value of 1. It returns *[[[ 1.   1.   0.], [ 0.   0.   0.]]]*.

Masking provides us with a simple implementation of MaskedLayer, which forms the base class that can be implemented by Masking layers for inheriting of boiler plate code. One can also extend the Masking layer to support a more advanced masking. To demonstrate this, we will create a masking layer to mask value above a particular value:

```
class CustomMasking(Masking):

  def get_output_mask(self, train=False):

    X = self.get_input(train)

    return K.any(K.ones_like(X) * (1. -

      K.equal(K.minimum(X, self.mask_value),

        self.mask_value)), axis=-1)


  def get_output(self, train=False):

    X = self.get_input(train)

    return X * K.any((1. - K.equal(

      K.minimum(X, self.mask_value),

        self.mask_value)), axis=-1, keepdims=True)


print_out(CustomMasking(mask_value=5),

  [[[3, 4, 5], [5, 6, 7], [5, 5, 5]]])
```

The code will return *[[[ 3. 4. 5.], [ 0. 0. 0.], [ 0. 0. 0.]]]*.

# Dropout

These layers work by turning off inputs in a bid to reduce over fitting. Note that dropout occurs only during over fitting. There is no need to turn off inputs during the test phase. The output values that are propagated forward, that is, not turned off, should increase in value to compensate for the nodes that are being turned off. Due to this, the value of the layer is just same with or with no dropout. Here is an example that helps make this clear:

**print_out(Dropout(.3), [1, 2, 3, 4, 5])**

The code will return *[0,0,0,5.71428585,7.14285755]*. This shows that with a dropout of 30%, a total of 3 output nodes were turned off, that is, set to 0. In order to compensate for output value of the layer, all other values have been increased accordingly. This has been done probabilistically so that they don't match the output exactly.

# Activation

An activation function works by applying an arbitrary function to input values of a layer to generate the output values of the layer. This function is expected to have a useful derivative since it is used during the backward/optimization step of the training. In neural networks, there are a number of activation functions. Examples include identity, binary step, logistic etc. Each of these formulas comes with a formula. Consider the following example were the activation function specified in the layer is applied to every input element solely to have arbitrary input data dimensions:

**print_out(Activation('tanh'), [.5, 1, 2, 3])**

**# It returns: [0.46211714,0.76159418,0.96402758,0.99505478]**

**print_out(Activation('softplus'), [.5, 1, 2, 3])**

**# It returns: [ 0.97407699  1.31326163  2.12692809 3.04858732]**

**print_out(Activation('relu'), [-2, -1, 0, 1, 2])**

# It returns: [ 0. 0. 0. 1. 2.]

print_out(Activation('sigmoid'), [.5, 1, 2, 3])

# It returns: [ 0.62245935 0.7310586 0.88079709 0.95257413]

print_out(Activation('hard_sigmoid'), [.5, 1, 2, 3])

# It returns: [ 0.60000002 0.69999999 0.89999998 1. ]

print_out(Activation('linear'), [.5, 1, 2, 3])

# It returns: [ 0.5 1. 2. 3. ] – no weights set


## Reshape

The purpose of this layer is to reshape an input into a new shape. However, you must note that the number of dimensions must remain the same. Consider the example given below:

print_out(Reshape(dims=(2,-1)), [[1, 2, 3, 4, 5, 6]])

# It returns: [[[ 1. 2. 3.], [ 4. 5. 6.]]]

print_out(Reshape(dims=(3,-1)), [[1, 2, 3, 4, 5, 6]])

# It returns: [[[ 1. 2.],[ 3. 4.],[ 5. 6.]]]

## Permute

To permute a tensor dimensions means to rearrange the dimensions. If for example we need to pivot a matrix, we can do the fo0llowing:

print_out(Permute(dims=(2,1)), [[[1, 2, 3],[4, 5, 6]]])

This will return *[[[ 1. 4.], [ 2. 5.], [ 3. 6.]]]*.

## Flatten

This works by flattening the rows of a 3D matrix. Here is an example:

**print_out(Flatten(), [[[1, 2, 3],[4, 5, 6]]])**

The code will return *[[ 1. 2. 3. 4. 5. 6.]]*.

## RepeatVector

This layer works by copying a 2D input matrix into a 3D matrix for n number of times. The following example demonstrates this:

**print_out(RepeatVector(2), [[1, 2, 3]])**

## Dense

A dense layer denotes a standard and fully connected neural network layer. Here is an example:

**d = Dense(3, init='uniform', activation='linear', input_dim=3)**

**d.set_weights([np.array([[.1, .2, .5], [.1, .2, .5], [.1, .2, .5]]),**

**np.array([0, 0, 0])])**

**print_out(d, [[10, 20, 30]])**

**# It returns: [[ 6. 12. 30.]]**

We passed an input of [10,20,30]. This was then converted into [6,12,30] by use of a linear activation layer and the weights of [.1,.2,.3] for every input row. If we take the last output node together with all the weights being 0.5 gives us an output of 30. The calculation can be done as follows:

**10*.5 + 20*.5 + 30*.5**

## TimeDistributedDense

This layer is similar to the standard Dense layer, with the difference being that in this case, we deal with an addition dimension of time. This means that the input and the output take the following shape:

(nb_sample, time_dimension, input_dim)

After we reproduce a dense example, we end up with the following:

**d = TimeDistributedDense(3, init='uniform',**

  **activation='linear', input_dim=3)**

**d.set_weights([np.array([[.1, .2, .5], [.1, .2, .5],**

  **[.1, .2, .5]]), np.array([0, 0, 0])])**

**print_out(d, [[[10, 20, 30]]])**

**# It returns: [[[ 6. 12. 30.]]]**

## Merge

This layer works by merging output obtained from various layers. It is commonly used when a Graph model needs recombining branches to form a single trunk. It is also used when there is a need to combine many models to get one model. The combination is done using strategies like sum, concat, mul, ave, and dot.

## TimeDistributedMerge

This layer converts a 3D output from a TimeDistributed layer into a 2D output with time steps merged by use any of the strategies which include sum, ave, mul. Here is an example:

**print_out(TimeDistributedMerge(mode='sum'), [[[1, 2, 3], [1, 2, 3]]])**

**# it returns: [[ 2. 4. 6.]]**

```
print_out(TimeDistributedMerge(mode='mul'), [[[1, 2, 3], [1, 2, 3]]])
```

# It returns: [[ 1.  4.  9.]]

```
print_out(TimeDistributedMerge(mode='ave'), [[[1, 2, 3], [1, 2, 3]]])
```

# It returns: [[ 1.  2.  3.]]

## ActivityRegularization

This acts as a wrapper around keras. Its work is applied regularization to loss functions. Here is an example:

```
r = ActivityRegularizer(l1=.01)

r.layer = Layer()

r.layer.input = np.array([1, 2, 3, 4, 5])

K.eval(r(0.))


r = ActivityRegularizer(l2=.01)

r.layer = Layer()

r.layer.input = np.array([1, 2, 3, 4, 5])

K.eval(r(0.))


r = ActivityRegularizer(l1=.01, l2=.01)

r.layer = Layer()

r.layer.input = np.array([1, 2, 3, 4, 5])
```

**K.eval(r(0.))**

## AutoEncoder

An auto encoder refers to an unsupervised neural network whose goal is to produce an output that is similar to your input data. This way, the neural network is able to learn more about the data as well as the regularization parameters without the use of labels. The output from the last is similar to the input of the first layer. It makes scoring simple since the row in the input is good for measuring the similarity of the produced output. The autoencoder is made up of two logical parts, the encoder that forms the layers of the neural network creating a hidden representation of the input data. Secondly, the decoder which has the layers of the neural network taking the produced presentation from encoder to create an output that should match the input data to your encoder. One of the advantages of using an auto encoder is that in case the hidden representation of the data becomes smaller than the input data, then the data will have been compressed, leading to dimensional reduction.

## Lambda

This one creates a layer to perform a python arbitrary function over the input data of the layers. For example:

**print_out(Lambda(lambda x: x*x), [1, 2, 3])**

**# It returns: [ 1.  4.  9.]**

## Convolutional Layers

## Conv1D

This layer simply creates a convolutional kernel with the layer input over single spatial or temporal dimension to generate a tensor of outputs. If the *use_bias* is true, a bias vector will be created then added to the outputs. If the activation is not None, it will also be applied to the outputs. If you decide to use this as the first layer in your model, make sure that you provide an *input_shape* argument (which is None or a tuple of integers not including the batch axis) for a time series sequence of 10-time steps with each step having 128 features. It is created as follows:

**keras.layers.Conv1D(filters, kernel_size, strides=1, padding='valid', data_format='channels_last', dilation_rate=1, activation=None, use_bias=True, kernel_initializer='glorot_uniform', bias_initializer='zeros', kernel_regularizer=None, bias_regularizer=None, activity_regularizer=None, kernel_constraint=None, bias_constraint=None)**

Here is a description of the above parameters:

- filters - Integer, showing the dimensionality of output space. It is the total number of output filters in a convolution.
- kernel_size - A tuple/list of a single integer or an integer stating the length of a 1D convolution window.
- strides - An integer or tuple/list of a single integer, stating the stride length of a convolution. Creating any stride value! = 1 is incompatible with creating any dilation_rate value! = 1.
- padding - it can be "valid", "causal" or "same" and it is case-insensitive. "valid" means there is "no padding". "same" will pad the input in such a way that the output has the similar length as its original input. "causal" leads into causal (dilated) convolutions, example, output[t] doesn't depend on input[t + 1:]. A zero padding is used so that the output has the similar length as original input. It is good during the modeling of temporal data in which the model shouldn't violate a temporal order.
- data_format - A string, and it is one of the "channels_last" or "channels_first", with the former being the default. Denotes the ordering of dimensions in the inputs. The "channels_last" corresponds to the inputs with the shape (batch, steps, channels) while the "channels_first" has inputs of the shape (batch, channels, steps).
- dilation_rate - this is an integer or a tuple/list of single integers, denoting the dilation rate to be used for a dilated convolution. Specifying a dilHere is the used description of the parameters:ation_rate value! = 1 is not compatible with specifying strides value != 1.

- activation - an activation function to be used. If nothing is specified, no activation will be applied (that is, "linear" activation: $a(x) = x$).
- use_bias - a Boolean stating whether the layer uses bias vector.
- kernel_initializer - an initializer for kernel weights matrix.
- bias_initializer - an initializer for bias vector.
- kernel_regularizer - a regularizer function that is applied to kernel weights matrix.
- bias_regularizer - a regularizer function that is applied to bias vector.
- activity_regularizer - a regularizer function that is applied to an output of a layer.
- kernel_constraint - a constraint function that is applied to kernel matrix.
- bias_constraint - a constraint function that is applied to bias vector.

The input is a 3D tensor with a shape of (batch, steps, and channels). The output is also a 3D tensor with the shape (batch, new_steps, and filters) (steps) and the value may have changed as a result of strides or padding.

## Conv2D

This layer works by creating a convolutional kernel with the layer input to generate a tensor of outputs. If the *use_bias* is true, then a bias vector will be created and added to outputs. If the *activation* is not None, it will also be applied to the outputs.

If need be you decide to use this layer as the first layer of your model, pass the *input_shape* keyword argument. For example, input_shape = (128, 128, 3) for a 128x128 RGB picture in *data_format="channels_last"*.

It is created as follows:

**keras.layers.Conv2D(filters, kernel_size, strides=(1, 1), padding='valid', data_format=None, dilation_rate=(1, 1), activation=None, use_bias=True, kernel_initializer='glorot_uniform', bias_initializer='zeros',**

**kernel_regularizer=None, bias_regularizer=None, activity_regularizer=None, kernel_constraint=None, bias_constraint=None)**

Here is the used description of the parameters:

- filters - Integer, showing the dimensionality of output space. It is the total number of output filters in a convolution.
- kernel_size - A tuple/list of 2 integers or an integer stating the length of a 2D convolution window.
- strides - An integer or tuple/list of 2 integers, stating the stride length of a convolution. Creating any stride value != 1 is incompatible with creating any dilation_rate value != 1.
- padding - it can be "valid", "causal" or "same" and it is case-insensitive. "valid" means there is "no padding". "same" will pad the input in such a way that the output has, Adam can be seen like the combination of RMSpropmilar length as its original input. "causal" leads into causal (dilated) convolutions, example, output[t] doesn't depend on input[t + 1:]. A zero padding is used so that the output has the similar length as original input. It is good during the modeling of temporal data in which the model shouldn't violate a temporal order.
- data_format - A string, and it is one of the "channels_last" or "channels_first", with the former being the default. Denotes the ordering of dimensions in the inputs. The "channels_last" corresponds to the inputs with the shape (batch, steps, channels) while the "channels_first" has inputs of the shape (batch, channels, steps).
- dilation_rate - this is an integer or a tuple/list of 2 integers, denoting the dilation rate to be used for a dilated convolution. Specifying a dilation_rate value != 1 is not compatible with specifying strides value != 1.
- Activation - an activation function to be used. If nothing is specified, no activation will be applied (that is, "linear" activation: a(x) = x).
- use_bias - a Boolean stating whether the layer uses bias vector.
- kernel_initializer - an initializer for kernel weights matrix.
- bias_initializer - an initializer for bias vector.
- kernel_regularizer - a regularizer function that is applied to kernel weights matrix.

- bias_regularizer - a regularizer function that is applied to bias vector.
- activity_regularizer - a regularizer function that is applied to an output of a layer.
- kernel_constraint - a constraint function that is applied to kernel matrix.
- bias_constraint - a constraint function that is applied to bias vector.

The input is a 4D tensor with a shape of (batch, channels, rows, cols) if the data_format is "channels_first" or a 4D tensor with the shape (batch, rows, cols, channels) if the data_format is "channels_last".

The output is a 4D tensor with a shape of (batch, filters, new_rows, new_cols) if the data_format is "channels_first" or a 4D tensor with the shape (batch, new_rows, new_cols, filters) if the data_format is "channels_last".

**SeparableConv1D**

In separable convolutions, a depth wise spatial convolution is performed first, acting on every input channel separately, and then followed by a point wise convolution that mixes the resulting output channels together. The argument depth multiplier is responsible for controlling the number of output channels that are generated for every input channel in depth wise step. They are created as follows:

**keras.layers.SeparableConv1D(filters, kernel_size, strides=1, padding='valid', data_format='channels_last', dilation_rate=1, depth_multiplier=1, activation=None, use_bias=True, depth wise_initializer='glorot_uniform', point wise_initializer='glorot_uniform', bias_initializer='zeros', depth wise_regularizer=None, point wise_regularizer=None, bias_regularizer=None, activity_regularizer=None, depth wise_constraint=None, point wise_constraint=None, bias_constraint=None)**

Here is the used description of the parameters:

- filters - Integer, showing the dimensional of output space. It is the total number of output filters in a convolution.

- kernel_size - A tuple/list of a single integer or an integer stating the length of a 1D convolution window.
- Strides - An integer or tuple/list of a single integer, stating the stride length of a convolution. Creating any stride value != 1 is incompatible with creating any dilation_rate value != 1.
- padding - it can be "valid", "causal" or "same" and it is case-insensitive. "valid" means there is "no padding". "same" will pad the input in such a way that the output has the similar length as its original input. "causal" leads into causal (dilated) convolutions, example, output[t] doesn't depend on input[t + 1:]. A zero padding is used so that the output has the similar length as original input. It is good during the modeling of temporal data in which the model shouldn't violate a temporal order.
- data_format - A string, and it is one of the "channels_last" or "channels_first", with the former being the default. Denotes the ordering of dimensions in the inputs. The "channels_last" corresponds to the inputs with the shape (batch, steps, channels) while the "channels_first" has inputs of the shape (batch, channels, steps).
- dilation_rate - this is an integer or a tuple/list of single integer, denoting the dilation rate to be used for a dilated convolution. Specifying a dilation_rate value != 1 is not compatible with specifying strides value != 1.
- activation - an activation function to be used. If nothing is specified, no activation will be applied (that is, "linear" activation: a(x) = x).
- use_bias - a Boolean stating whether the layer uses bias vector.
- kernel_initializer - an initializer for kernel weights matrix.
- bias_initializer - an initializer for bias vector.
- kernel_regularizer - a regularizer function that is applied to kernel weights matrix.
- bias_regularizer - a regularizer function that is applied to bias vector.
- activity_regularizer - a regularizer function that is applied to an output of a layer.
- kernel_constraint - a constraint function that is applied to kernel matrix.
- bias_constraint - a constraint function that is applied to bias vector.

The input is a 3D tensor of shape (batch, channels, steps) if the data_format is "channels_first" or a 3D tensor with the shape (batch, steps, channels) if the data_format is "channels_last". The output is a 3D tensor of shape (batch, filters, new_steps) if the data_format is "channels_first" or a 3D tensor with the shape (batch, new_steps, filters) if the data_format is "channels_last".

**SeparableConv2D**

In separable convolutions, a depth wise spatial convolution is performed first, acting on every input channel separately, and then followed by a point wise convolution that mixes the resulting output channels together.

The argument depth multiplier is responsible for controlling the number of output channels that are generated for every input channel in depth wise step. They are created as follows:

**keras.layers.SeparableConv2D(filters, kernel_size, strides=(1, 1), padding='valid', data_format=None, dilation_rate=(1, 1), depth_multiplier=1, activation=None, use_bias=True, depth wise_initializer='glorot_uniform', point wise_initializer='glorot_uniform', bias_initializer='zeros', depth wise_regularizer=None, point wise_regularizer=None, bias_regularizer=None, activity_regularizer=None, depth wise_constraint=None, point wise_constraint=None, bias_constraint=None)**

The following parameters have been used:

- filters - Integer, showing the dimensional of output space. It is the total number of output filters in a convolution.
- kernel_size - A tuple/list of a single integer or an integer stating the length of a 2D convolution window.
- strides - An integer or tuple/list of 2 integers, stating the stride length of a convolution. Creating any stride value != 1 is incompatible with creating any dilation_rate value != 1.
- padding - it can be "valid", "causal" or "same" and it is case-insensitive. "valid" means there is "no padding". "same" will pad the input in such a way that the output has the similar length as its

original input. "causal" leads into causal (dilated) convolutions, example, output[t] doesn't depend on input[t + 1:]. A zero padding is used so that the output has the similar length as original input. It is good during the modeling of temporal data in which the model shouldn't violate a temporal order.

- data_format - A string, and it is one of the "channels_last" or "channels_first", with the former being the default. Denotes the ordering of dimensions in the inputs. The "channels_last" corresponds to the inputs with the shape (batch, steps, channels) while the "channels_first" has inputs of the shape (batch, channels, steps).

- dilation_rate - this is an integer or a tuple/list of 2 integers, denoting the dilation rate to be used for a dilated convolution. Specifying a dilation_rate value != 1 is not compatible with specifying strides value != 1.

- activation - an activation function to be used. If nothing is specified, no activation will be applied (that is, "linear" activation: $a(x) = x$).

- use_bias - a Boolean stating whether the layer uses bias vector.

- kernel_initializer - an initializer for kernel weights matrix.

- bias_initializer - an initializer for bias vector.

- kernel_regularizer - a regularizer function that is applied to kernel weights matrix.

- bias_regularizer - a regularizer function that is applied to bias vector.

- activity_regularizer - a regularizer function that is applied to an output of a layer.

- kernel_constraint - a constraint function that is applied to kernel matrix.

- bias_constraint - a constraint function that is applied to bias vector.

**Pooling Layers**

**MaxPooling1D**

This layer performs a max pooling operation for some temporal data. It is created as follows:

**keras.layers.MaxPooling1D(pool_size=2, strides=None, padding='valid', data_format='channels_last')**

Here is the used description of the parameters:

- pool_size - an integer that denotes the size of max pooling windows.
- strides - an integer, or None. It is the factor by which we will downscale. For example, 2 will have the effect of halving the input. If None, then it will default to the pool_size.
- Padding - one of "valid" or "same", it is case-insensitive.
- data_forma t- this is a string, one of the channels_last (default) or channels_first. It denotes the ordering of dimensions in the inputs. The channels_last corresponds to the inputs with a shape of (batch, steps, features) while the channels_first corresponds to the inputs with a shape of (batch, features, steps).

If data_format='channels_last', its input is a 3D tensor with a shape of (batch_size, steps, features).

If data_format='channels_first', the input is a 3D tensor with a shape of (batch_size, features, steps). For the case of the output, if data_format='channels_last', it is a 3D tensor with a shape of (batch_size, downsampled_steps, features).

If data_format='channels_first', the output is a 3D tensor with a shape of (batch_size, features, downsampled_steps).

## MaxPooling2D

This layer performs a max pooling operation on spatial data. It is created as follows:

**keras.layers.MaxPooling2D(pool_size=(2, 2), strides=None, padding='valid', data_format=None)**

The parameters are described below:

- pool_size - an integer or a tuple of 2 integers that denotes the factor by which we will downscale.

- strides - an integer, or None. It is the factor by which we will downscale. For example, 2 will have the effect of halving the input. If None, then it will default to the pool_size.
- padding - one of "valid" or "same", it is case-insensitive.
- data_format - this is a string, one of the channels_last (default) or channels_first. It denotes the ordering of dimensions in the inputs. The channels_last corresponds to the inputs with a shape of (batch, steps, features) while the channels_first corresponds to the inputs with a shape of (batch, features, steps).

If data_format='channels_last', the input is a 4D tensor with a shape of (batch_size, rows, cols, channels). If data_format='channels_first', the input will be a 4D tensor with a shape of (batch_size, channels, rows, cols). If data_format='channels_last', the output is a 4D tensor with a shape of (batch_size, pooled_rows, pooled_cols, channels). If data_format='channels_first', the output is a 4D tensor with a shape of (batch_size, channels, pooled_rows, pooled_cols).

Other layers in this category include MaxPooling3D, AveragePooling1D, AveragePooling2D, AveragePooling3D, GlobalMaxPooling1D, GlobalAveragePooling1D, GlobalMaxPooling2D, GlobalAveragePooling2D, GlobalMaxPooling3D and GlobalAveragePooling3D.

### Locally-connected Layers

### LocallyConnected1D

This is a locally connected layer for 1D input. This type of layer works in the same way as a Conv1D layer, but the weights are not shared, but a different set of filters is used for every different patch of inputs.

It can be created as follows:

**keras.layers.LocallyConnected1D(filters, kernel_size, strides=1, padding='valid', data_format=None, activation=None, use_bias=True, kernel_initializer='glorot_uniform', bias_initializer='zeros',**

kernel_regularizer=None, bias_regularizer=None,
activity_regularizer=None, kernel_constraint=None,
bias_constraint=None)

Here is an example:

# apply unshared weight convolution 1d with a length of 3 to a sequence

# of 10 timesteps and 64 output filters

model = Sequential()

model.add(LocallyConnected1D(64, 3, input_shape=(10, 32)))

# now model.output_shape == (None, 8, 64)

# add new conv1d

model.add(LocallyConnected1D(32, 3))

# now model.output_shape == (None, 6, 32)

The input is a 3D tensor with a shape of (batch_size, steps, input_dim). The output is a 3D tensor with a shape of (batch_size, new_steps, filters) (steps).

**LocallyConnected2D**

This is a locally connected layer of 2D inputs. It works similarly as the Conv2D layer but the weights are not shared since a different set of filters is applied at every different patch of input.

It is created as follows:

keras.layers.LocallyConnected2D(filters, kernel_size, strides=(1, 1), padding='valid', data_format=None, activation=None, use_bias=True, kernel_initializer='glorot_uniform', bias_initializer='zeros', kernel_regularizer=None, bias_regularizer=None, activity_regularizer=None, kernel_constraint=None, bias_constraint=None)

For example:

# apply 3x3 unshared weights convolution having 64 output filters

# on 32x32 image with `data_format="channels_last"`:

model = Sequential()

model.add(LocallyConnected2D(64, (3, 3), input_shape=(32, 32, 3)))

# now model.output_shape == (None, 30, 30, 64)

# the layer will consume (30*30)*(3*3*3*64)

# + (30*30)*64 parameters


# add 3x3 unshared weights convolution, with 32 output filters:

model.add(LocallyConnected2D(32, (3, 3)))

# now model.output_shape == (None, 28, 28, 32)

If data_format='channels_first', the input is a 4D tensor with a shape of (samples, channels, rows, cols). If data_format='channels_last', the input is a 4D tensor with a shape of (samples, rows, cols, channels).

If data_format='channels_first', the output is a 4D tensor with a shape of (samples, filters, new_rows, new_cols). If data_format='channels_last', the output is a 4D tensor with a shape of (samples, new_rows, new_cols, filters).

## Recurrent Layers

### RNN

This forms the base class for recurrent layers. It can be created as follows:

**keras.layers.RNN(cell, return_sequences=False, return_state=False, go_backwards=False, stateful=False, unroll=False)**

The input is a 3D tensor with a shape of (batch_size, timesteps, input_dim).

If return_state, the output is a list of tensors, with the first tensor forming the output and the rest of the tensors form the last states, each with a shape of (batch_size, units). If return_sequences, the output is a 3D tensor with a shape of (batch_size, timesteps, units). Else, the output is a 2D tensor with a shape of (batch_size, units).

Note that you can pass external constants to an RNN. This can be done by use of the *constants* keyword argument of the *RNN.__ call__* method. The following example demonstrates this:

*# We first define a RNN Cell to be a layer subclass.*

```python
class MinimalRNNCell(keras.layers.Layer):


    def __init__(self, units, **kwargs):

        self.units = units

        self.state_size = units

        super(MinimalRNNCell, self).__init__(**kwargs)
```

```python
    def build(self, input_shape):

        self.kernel = self.add_weight(shape=(input_shape[-1],
self.units),
                                      initializer='uniform',
                                      name='kernel')
        self.recurrent_kernel = self.add_weight(
            shape=(self.units, self.units),
            initializer='uniform',
            name='recurrent_kernel')
        self.built = True


    def call(self, inputs, states):
        prev_output = states[0]
        h = K.dot(inputs, self.kernel)
        output = h + K.dot(prev_output, self.recurrent_kernel)
        return output, [output]


# We then use the cell in RNN layer:


cell = MinimalRNNCell(32)
x = keras.Input((None, 5))
layer = RNN(cell)
```

```
y = layer(x)
```

*# Let's use the cell to create a stacked RNN:*

```
cells = [MinimalRNNCell(32), MinimalRNNCell(64)]

x = keras.Input((None, 5))

layer = RNN(cells)

y = layer(x)
```

SimpleRNN

This is a fully connected RNN in which the output is fed back to the network as the input. It is created as follows:

```
keras.layers.SimpleRNN(units, activation='tanh',
use_bias=True, kernel_initializer='glorot_uniform',
recurrent_initializer='orthogonal', bias_initializer='zeros',
kernel_regularizer=None, recurrent_regularizer=None,
bias_regularizer=None, activity_regularizer=None,
kernel_constraint=None, recurrent_constraint=None,
bias_constraint=None, dropout=0.0, recurrent_dropout=0.0,
return_sequences=False, return_state=False,
go_backwards=False, stateful=False, unroll=False)
```

Other Keras layers are Embedding layers, Merge layers, Advanced activation layers, Normalization layers and Noise layers.

## Learning Rate

Training a neural network or a deep learning model can be a difficult task. The standard algorithm used for training neural networks is known as *stochastic gradient descent*. It has been found that one can achieve an increased performance and a faster training on certain problems by use of a learning rate that is capable of changing over time. Using an optimal learning rate for your stochastic gradient descent optimization procedure can reduce the training time and improve performance. The purpose of learning rate schedules is to adjust the learning rate during the training of a neural network. Let us discuss how these can be used with the Keras library:

### Time-Based Learning Rate Schedule

The keras library comes with a time-based learning schedule built-in. The implementation of the stochastic gradient descent optimization algorithm in SGD class has an argument named *decay*. We can use this argument in the time-based learning rate decay schedule equation as shown below:

**LearningRate = LearningRate * 1/(1 + decay * epoch)**

When the value of the decay argument is 0, which is also the default value, it means that there will be no effect on learning rate as shown below:

**LearningRate = 0.1 * 1/(1 + 0.0 * 1)**

**LearningRate = 0.1**

If you specify the decay argument, the learning rate will be decreased from the previous epoch by the fixed amount that is specified.

If for example we use a learning rate 0.1 and a decay of 0.001, the learning rate will be adapted as follows for the first 5 epochs:

**Epoch Learning Rate**

1   0.1

2   0.0999000999

3   0.0997006985

4   0.09940249103

5   0.09900646517

If you extend this to around 100 epochs, you will get a graph line that shows a reduction of learning rate with each epoch.

You can come up with a nice default schedule by setting your decay value as shown below:

**Decay = LearningRate / Epochs**

**Decay = 0.1 / 100**

**Decay = 0.001**

We need to create an example that demonstrates how to use the time-based learning rate schedule in Keras. We will use the Ionosphere binary classification problem. The dataset can be obtained from the following URL:

**http://archive.ics.uci.edu/ml/machine-learning-databases/ionosphere/ionosphere.data**

Download the dataset and save it in a file named ionosphere.csv. We will create a small neural network model with one hidden layer and 34 neurons and use the rectifier activation function. The output layer will have only one neuron and it will use the sigmoid activation function to generate probability-like values. We will use a higher rate for the learning rate of stochastic gradient descent, 0.1. A decay argument of 0.002 (0.1/50) will be used and training will be done for 50 epochs.

Momentum is also good when using adaptive learning rate. Let us use a momentum of 0.8. Ensure that you save the data above in the same directory as the file with this code:

```
import numpy

from keras.models import Sequential

from pandas import read_csv

from keras.layers import Dense

from sklearn.preprocessing import LabelEncoder

from keras.optimizers import SGD

# fix a random seed for reproducibility

seed = 7

numpy.random.seed(seed)

# load the dataset

dataframe = read_csv("ionosphere.csv", header=None)

dataset = dataframe.values

# split the dataset into input (X) and output (Y) variables

X = dataset[:,0:34].astype(float)

Y = dataset[:,34]

# encode the class values as integers

encoder = LabelEncoder()

encoder.fit(Y)

Y = encoder.transform(Y)
```

```
# create a model

model = Sequential()

model.add(Dense(34, input_dim=34,
kernel_initializer='normal', activation='relu'))

model.add(Dense(1, kernel_initializer='normal',
activation='sigmoid'))

# Compile the model

epochs = 50

learning_rate = 0.1

decay_rate = learning_rate / epochs

momentum = 0.8

sgd = SGD(lr=learning_rate, momentum=momentum,
decay=decay_rate, nesterov=False)

model.compile(loss='binary_crossentropy', optimizer=sgd,
metrics=['accuracy'])

# Fit the model

model.fit(X,Y,validation_split=0.33, epochs=epochs,
batch_size=28, verbose=2)
```

We have used 67% of the dataset to train the model and 33% of the dataset to test/validate the model. The code runs with an accuracy of 99.14%, which is higher compared to a baseline of 95.69% without the use of a learning rate decay or momentum.

## Drop-Based Learning Rate Schedule

With this schedule, the learning rate is dropped systematically at certain times during the training. The method is implemented in such a way that the learning rate is dropped by half after each fixed number of epochs. For example, we can start with a learning rate of 0.1 then we drop it by 0.5 after every 10 epochs. The first 10 epochs for which we train the model will use a learning rate of 0.1, the next 10 epochs will use a learning rate of 0.05 and this continues. This can be implemented in Keras by use of the LearningRateScheduler callback at the time of fitting of the model. With this callback, we can define a function that takes an epoch number as the argument and it in turn returns a learning rate to be used in the stochastic gradient descent. When this is used, the learning rate that is specified in the stochastic gradient descent will be ignored.

We will use the previous dataset of Ionosphere and create a network of a single hidden layer. We have created a new function named *step_decay()* to implement the following equation:

**LearningRate = InitialLearningRate * DropRate^floor(Epoch / EpochDrop)**

The InitialLearningRate denotes the initial learning, which is a value such as 0.1, the DropRate denotes the amount by which we will modify the learning rate each time it is changed such as 0.5, and the Epoch is the number of the current epoch while the EpochDrop denotes how often we will change the learning rate like 10.

The learning rate has been set to 0, which means that we will not be using it. However, if you need to use a momentum, you can set it. The code for the drop-based learning rate schedule is given below:

**import pandas**

**import numpy**

**import math**

**from pandas import read_csv**

```python
from keras.models import Sequential

from keras.optimizers import SGD

from keras.layers import Dense

from keras.callbacks import LearningRateScheduler

from sklearn.preprocessing import LabelEncoder


# the learning rate schedule

def step_decay(epoch):

        initial_lrate = 0.1

        drop = 0.5

        epochs_drop = 10.0

        lrate = initial_lrate * math.pow(drop,
math.floor((1+epoch)/epochs_drop))

        return lrate


# fix a random seed for reproducibility

seed = 7

numpy.random.seed(seed)

# load the dataset

dataframe = read_csv("ionosphere.csv", header=None)

dataset = dataframe.values

# split the dataset into input (X) and output (Y) variables
```

```python
X = dataset[:,0:34].astype(float)

Y = dataset[:,34]

# encode the class values as integers

encoder = LabelEncoder()

encoder.fit(Y)

Y = encoder.transform(Y)

# create the model

model = Sequential()

model.add(Dense(34, input_dim=34,
kernel_initializer='normal', activation='relu'))

model.add(Dense(1, kernel_initializer='normal',
activation='sigmoid'))

# Compile the model

sgd = SGD(lr=0.0, momentum=0.9, decay=0.0,
nesterov=False)

model.compile(loss='binary_crossentropy', optimizer=sgd,
metrics=['accuracy'])

# the learning schedule callback

lrate = LearningRateScheduler(step_decay)

callbacks_list = [lrate]

# Fit a model

model.fit(X, Y, validation_split=0.33, epochs=50,
batch_size=28, callbacks=callbacks_list, verbose=2)
```

The code gives me an accuracy of 99.14% upon execution on the test/validation dataset. This is also higher when compared to the baseline for the model.

**Exponential Decay**

This learning schedule takes the mathematical equation given below:

**lr = lr0 * e^(−kt)**

In the above equation, *lr* and *k* are hyperparameters while *t* denotes the iterator number. It can also be implemented by defining an exponential decay function and passing it to the *learningRatescheduler*. In fact, we can use this approach to define any custom decay schedule in Keras library. The difference will come in defining a different custom decay function.

```
def exp_decay(epoch):
    initial_lrate = 0.1
    k = 0.1
    lrate = initial_lrate * exp(-k*t)
    return lrate

lrate = LearningRateScheduler(exp_decay)
```

**keras optimizers**

Each time that a neural network has finished passing a batch through a network and generated prediction results, it has to decide about what to do about the difference between the obtained results and the true values so that the weights to the network must be adjusted towards meeting a solution. This step is determined using an algorithm known as the *optimization algorithm.*

Keras comes with many optimization algorithms. Let us discuss how these can be used:

Don't forget that for you to use Keras you must import it using the *import* statement as shown below:

**import keras**

## SGD

This stands for *Stochastic Gradient Descent* and it is a classical optimization algorithm. In this algorithm, the gradient of the network loss function is calculated in relation to every individual weight in the network. Every forward pass through the network leads to a particular parameterized loss function, and the gradients we have created are used for each weight, and then multiplied by a particular learning rate to move the weights in the direction that the gradient is pointing. SGD can be said to be the simplest algorithm in terms of concepts and behavior. When this algorithm is given a small learning rate, it will follow the gradient on the cost surface. The new weights that are generated after iteration are always better compared to the previous ones.

Due to the simplicity of the SGD algorithm, it has become very good for shallow networks. However, you should also note that the SGD algorithm converges a bit slowly compared to other more advanced algorithms that we have in Keras. It also has the least capability to escape the locally optimal traps that are available in cost surface. That is why the SGD algorithm is not commonly used in the deep networks. It can be accessed from the following:

**keras.optimizers.SGD**

There are various parameters that are implemented by the SGD algorithm.

### SGD with (Nesterov) Momentum

The Nesterov momentum is one of the parameters that made algorithms converge faster. The technique uses momentum. Momentum techniques work by introducing information from the previous steps to decide in the current step. This means that descent in an algorithm will not rely only on the current determination of the algorithm but also on some steps that it undertaken previously.

Momentum has an advantage. It helps in handling a problem that is common when using the straight SGD, which is the problem of local minima traps. If the local minimum is wide enough to push a gradient step back to itself, the SGD may get stuck. With momentum, the learner can jump and avoid the local minima. Momentum techniques also have another advantage in that optimizers are able to learn much quickly, which is achieved by selecting larger learning rates.

One of the best ways to apply iteration is for iteration made by the learner, we create a vector of decaying average of the past steps that were taken by the algorithm, sum them with the vector of the current gradient, then take the direction of the summed vector.

The Nesterov momentum varies this approach slightly for better results. It takes in a decayed average of the previous steps and the steps in that direction first. Next, we calculate the gradient from the new position by use of our data and we perform a correction. The weights are thus updated twice for iteration, first using momentum and secondly using our gradient algorithm.

This explains why the Nesterov momentum is better compared to the simple momentum. It uses additional information, which is the gradient of the data at uncorrected point.

By default, SGD doesn't use momentum. However, if you need to use momentum or Nesterov momentum, you can configure it as shown below:

**keras.optimizers.SGD(momentum=0.01, nesterov=True)**

## Adagrad

This is an advanced machine learning technique that performs gradient descent using a variable learning rate. The node weights that were known to have large gradients are assigned large gradients, while node weights that were known to have small gradients are assigned small gradients.

This means that Adagrad is an effective SGD when used with a per-node learning rate scheduler that is built into the algorithm. Adagrad improves SGD by providing weights with learning rates that are historically accurate instead of relying on a single learning rate for all the nodes. Adagrad can be **assessed** as follows:

**keras.optimizers.adagrad**

## Adadelta

This is a kind of Adagrad that relies on momentum techniques to handle the problem of monotonically decreasing learning rate. In Adadelta, the gradient update on every weight is a weighted sum of the current gradient and exponentially decaying average composed of a limited number of the past gradient updates. The gradient denominator in this case is not monotonically decreasing, hence the learning rate becomes more stable, and the overall algorithm becomes more robust.

In its first implementation, Adadelta required no learning rate parameter to be setup. However, the Keras library comes with modified version of Adadelta with a defined learning rate that is in consistency with the other Keras optimization algorithms. We can adadelta in Keras as follows:

**keras.optimizers.adadelta**

## RMSprop

This optimizer is a correction of Adagrad proposed independently of the adadelta optimizer. It is similar to Adadelta with the difference being that the learning rate has been divided further using an exponentially decaying average for all squared gradients, that is, global tuning value.

It is recommended that you leave the hyper parameters of this optimization algorithm in their default setting. It can be **assessed** as follows within the Keras library:

**keras.optimizers.rmsprop**

## Adam (Adaptive Moment Estimation)

Just like RMSprop and Adadelta, it stores an exponentially decaying average of the past squared gradients. In addition to this, it stores an exponentially decaying average of decaying average of the past gradients, just like momentum.

Adam can be seen like the combination of RMSprop and momentum. It follows a path that is similar to the one of a ball with friction and momentum. Adam adds bias to the path followed by the algorithm towards a flat minimum on the error surface, with learning be made slow when moving on a large gradient.

Adam is currently amongst the popular optimization algorithms, which can be attributed to the fact that it provides a smart learning rate annealing as well as the momentum behaviors that it provides. It can be assessed as follows:

**keras.optimizers.adam**

## AdaMax

Just like RMSprop and other optimization algorithms, this algorithm relies on an exponentially decaying weighted average obtained from the variance of the gradient in the formulation. However, there is no requirement for us to use the variance.

The variance is similar to the L2 norm or second moment of the gradient. When compared to Adam, Adamax shows more robustness to gradient update noise and it has a better numerical stability. It can be **assessed** as follows:

**keras.optimizers.adamax**

# Nadam

Nadam is similar to Adam, but with Nesterov momentum rather than the ordinary momentum. The use of the Nesterov momentum in place of the ordinary momentum has a similar advantage as it is the case in SGD. This optimizer can be assessed as follows:

**keras.optimizers.nadam**

# AMSgrad

This forms the recent proposal for improvement of the Adam optimizer algorithm. It was found that with some datasets, Adam doesn't converge to a globally optimal solution, but simple algorithms like SGD do. It has been hypothesized that in some datasets such as those for image recognition, there is small, less informative gradients that are caused by the occasional large and more informative gradients. Adam comes with an inbuilt tendency to deprioritize more informative gradients since such are swallowed quickly by those weighting exponentially, making the algorithm to steer beyond the optimality point without exploring it sufficiently.

This algorithm has been found to perform very well on certain datasets, but it is yet to displace Adam due to its lack of verifiability when it comes to win on general-purpose datasets. It can be assessed as follows:

**keras.optimizers.adam(amsgrad=True)**

# Cost Functions

The training of deep learning neural networks is done using stochastic gradient descent optimization algorithm. During training, the error of any current state of the model should be assessed repeatedly. This requires one to use an error function, mostly referred to as a *loss function*. This function can be used for evaluating the loss made by a model so that the weights can be adjusted appropriately to reduce the loss during the next evaluation.

Neural networks map inputs to outputs and the chosen loss function should match the framing of a certain predictive modeling problem like regression or classification. Also, the output layer must also be configured well to match how the loss function has been configured.

**Regression Loss Functions**

In regression predictive modeling, we predict real-valued quantities. We will be discussing the loss functions that are appropriate for such problems.

We will be using the standard regression problem generator provided by the scikit-learn library in *make_regression()* problem. This function works by generating examples from a very simple regression problem with a particular number of input variables, statistical noise as well as other properties.

The function will be used for definition of a problem with 20 input features, where 10 of these features will be relevant but the remaining 10 will not be relevant. We will randomly generate 1000 examples. We will use a fixed pseudorandom number generator to ensure that the code generates 1000 examples each time it is executed. This is shown below:

**# generate a regression dataset**

**X, y = make_regression(n_samples=1000, n_features=20, noise=0.1, random_state=1)**

Neural networks exhibit a better performance when the goal is to scale real-valued input and output variables to sensible range. In this problem, each input and target variables have a Gaussian distribution, making it desirable to standardize data in this case.

This can be achieved by use of the StandardScaler transform class provided by the scikit-learn library. If this was a real problem, we would have prepared the scaler on a standard dataset then apply it to the train and test sets. However, to make things simple, we will be scaling all our data together before we can split it into train and test sets.

---

# standardize the dataset

X = StandardScaler().fit_transform(X)

y = StandardScaler().fit_transform(y.reshape(len(y),1))[:,0]

Now that the data has been scaled, we can split it into the two sets:

# split data into train and test

n_train = 500

trainX, testX = X[:n_train, :], X[n_train:, :]

trainy, testy = y[:n_train], y[n_train:]

We will define a small Multilayer Perceptron model to address this problem and give the basis as to why different loss functions should be explored.

The model will be expecting 20 features as the input as we defined. Our model will consist of one hidden with a total of 25 nodes and the rectified linear activation function will be used. The output layer will have only 1 node since only one real-value is to be predicted, and it will rely on a linear activation function.

# define the model

model = Sequential()

model.add(Dense(25, input_dim=20, activation='relu', kernel_initializer='he_uniform'))

model.add(Dense(1, activation='linear'))

We now need to fit the model using a stochastic gradient descent and a learning rate of 0.01 and momentum of 0.9, all being sensible default values. We need to do the training for a total of 100n epochs and the test dataset will have to be evaluated at the end of every epoch.

This will help in the generation of learning curves at the end of the process.

```
opt = SGD(lr=0.01, momentum=0.9)
```

```
model.compile(loss='...', optimizer=opt)
```

```
# fit the model
```

```
history = model.fit(trainX, trainy, validation_data=(testX, testy), epochs=100, verbose=0)
```

At this point, we have defined our model; hence we can go ahead and evaluate three loss functions that are appropriate for regression predictive modeling problems.

## Mean Squared Error Loss

The MSE is the default loss used for regression problems.

Mathematically, it is the recommended loss function under inference framework of maximum likelihood if the target variable has a Gaussian distribution. This loss function should be evaluated first and changed only in cases where there is a good reason.

To calculate MSE, we get the average of the squared differences between predicted and actual values. The obtained result is always a positive value and with the perfect value being 0.0. Since there is squaring, it means that larger mistakes lead into big errors compared to smaller mistakes.

To use the mean squared error loss function in Keras, we specify the "mse" or "mean_squared_error" as the loss function during the time of compiling the model. This is shown below:

```
model.compile(loss='mean_squared_error')
```

We recommend that you use one node for the output layer for the target variable and use a linear activation function:

```
model.add(Dense(1, activation='linear'))
```

The following is a complete example demonstrating how to use MLP on a regression problem:

```
# mlp for regression and mse loss function

from sklearn.preprocessing import StandardScaler

from sklearn.datasets import make_regression

from keras.models import Sequential

from keras.optimizers import SGD

from keras.layers import Dense

from matplotlib import pyplot

# generate a regression dataset

X, y = make_regression(n_samples=1000, n_features=20,
noise=0.1, random_state=1)

# standardize the dataset

X = StandardScaler().fit_transform(X)

y = StandardScaler().fit_transform(y.reshape(len(y),1))[:,0]

# split the dataset into train and test sets

n_train = 500

trainX, testX = X[:n_train, :], X[n_train:, :]

trainy, testy = y[:n_train], y[n_train:]

# define the model

model = Sequential()
```

```python
model.add(Dense(25, input_dim=20, activation='relu',
kernel_initializer='he_uniform'))

model.add(Dense(1, activation='linear'))

opt = SGD(lr=0.01, momentum=0.9)

model.compile(loss='mean_squared_error', optimizer=opt)

# fit the model

history = model.fit(trainX, trainy, validation_data=(testX,
testy), epochs=100, verbose=0)

# evaluate model

train_mse = model.evaluate(trainX, trainy, verbose=0)

test_mse = model.evaluate(testX, testy, verbose=0)

print('Train: %.3f, Test: %.3f' % (train_mse, test_mse))

# plot the loss during training

pyplot.title('Loss / Mean Squared Error')

pyplot.plot(history.history['loss'], label='train')

pyplot.plot(history.history['val_loss'], label='test')

pyplot.legend()

pyplot.show()
```

If the above model is executed, it will return the mean squared error for both the train and the test datasets.

Since the training algorithm is stochastic, the specific results may differ. That is why you execute the code for a number of times. In my case, I get the following:

**Train: 0.000, Test: 0.001**

This means that the model learned the problem and achieved an error of zero, to three decimal places. The generated line plot shows that the model converged quickly with the train and test performances remaining the same. This convergence and performance behavior exhibited by the model shows that the mean squared error is a good for a neural network that tries to learn this problem.

**Mean Squared Logarithmic Error Loss**

We may encounter regression problems in which the target value is composed of a spread of values and when you need to predict a large value, you may not need to punish the model as heavily as the mean squared error.

Instead of this, you can begin by calculating the natural algorithm for each predicted value, and then we determine the mean square error. This is referred to as the Mean Squared Logarithmic Error loss or MSLE in short. Its effect is relaxing the punished effect associated with large differences in large predicted values.

Since it is a measure of loss, it can be appropriate to use the model to predict unscaled quantities directly. We can create a demonstration of this loss function by use of a simple regression problem. We can update our model to use a mean_squared_logarithmic_error loss function then we maintain the same configuration for the output layer. The mean square error will also be tracked as a metric during fitting of the model and use it as a metric to measure performance and plot a curve:

**model.compile(loss='mean_squared_logarithmic_error', optimizer=opt, metrics=['mse'])**

The following code demonstrates how we can use the MSLE loss function:

**# mlp for regression and a msle loss function**

**from sklearn.preprocessing import StandardScaler**

```python
from sklearn.datasets import make_regression

from keras.models import Sequential

from keras.optimizers import SGD

from keras.layers import Dense

from matplotlib import pyplot

# generate a regression dataset

X, y = make_regression(n_samples=1000, n_features=20,
noise=0.1, random_state=1)

# standardize the dataset

X = StandardScaler().fit_transform(X)

y = StandardScaler().fit_transform(y.reshape(len(y),1))[:,0]

# split the dataset into train and test sets

n_train = 500

trainX, testX = X[:n_train, :], X[n_train:, :]

trainy, testy = y[:n_train], y[n_train:]

# define a model

model = Sequential()

model.add(Dense(25, input_dim=20, activation='relu',
kernel_initializer='he_uniform'))

model.add(Dense(1, activation='linear'))

opt = SGD(lr=0.01, momentum=0.9)
```

```python
model.compile(loss='mean_squared_logarithmic_error',
optimizer=opt, metrics=['mse'])

# fit the model

history = model.fit(trainX, trainy, validation_data=(testX,
testy), epochs=100, verbose=0)

# evaluate the model

_, train_mse = model.evaluate(trainX, trainy, verbose=0)

_, test_mse = model.evaluate(testX, testy, verbose=0)

print('Train: %.3f, Test: %.3f' % (train_mse, test_mse))

# plot the loss during training

pyplot.subplot(211)

pyplot.title('Loss')

pyplot.plot(history.history['loss'], label='train')

pyplot.plot(history.history['val_loss'], label='test')

pyplot.legend()

# plot the mse during training

pyplot.subplot(212)

pyplot.title('Mean Squared Error')

pyplot.plot(history.history['mean_squared_error'],
label='train')

pyplot.plot(history.history['val_mean_squared_error'],
label='test')

pyplot.legend()
```

**pyplot.show()**

The code will return the mean square error of the model on your train and test sets.

The training algorithm is stochastic in nature, which means that you may get varying results. Just run the code for a number of times.

From the obtained results, the model gave us a slightly worse MSE for the datasets, that is, the train and the test datasets. Due to this, it may not fit our problem since the target variable is a standard Gaussian. This is the result I got:

**Train: 0.165, Test: 0.184**

From the line plot, it is clear that the MSLE converged very well for the first 100 epochs of the algorithm, which indicates that the MSE may be showing signs of over fitting the problem, dropping very fast then beginning to rise from epoch 20 and onwards.

**Mean Absolute Error Loss (MAE)**

For a number of regression problems, the target variable may mostly have a Gaussian distribution, but it can have outliers, like values that are too far from the mean in terms of size.

The MAE loss is a good loss function for this case since it shows more robustness as far as outliers are concerned. To calculate it, we get the average of absolute difference between the predicted and the actual values.

We can update the model to use the mean_absolute_error function, but we maintain the same configuration for the output layer:

**model.compile(loss='mean_absolute_error', optimizer=opt, metrics=['mse'])**

The following example demonstrates how to use the mean absolute error as the loss function in a regression problem:

**# mlp for regression with mae as the loss function**

```python
from sklearn.preprocessing import StandardScaler

from sklearn.datasets import make_regression

from keras.models import Sequential

from keras.optimizers import SGD

from keras.layers import Dense

from matplotlib import pyplot

# generate a regression dataset

X, y = make_regression(n_samples=1000, n_features=20,
noise=0.1, random_state=1)

# standardize the dataset

X = StandardScaler().fit_transform(X)

y = StandardScaler().fit_transform(y.reshape(len(y),1))[:,0]

# split the dataset into train and test sets

n_train = 500

trainX, testX = X[:n_train, :], X[n_train:, :]

trainy, testy = y[:n_train], y[n_train:]

# define the model

model = Sequential()

model.add(Dense(25, input_dim=20, activation='relu',
kernel_initializer='he_uniform'))

model.add(Dense(1, activation='linear'))

opt = SGD(lr=0.01, momentum=0.9)
```

```python
model.compile(loss='mean_absolute_error', optimizer=opt,
metrics=['mse'])

# fit the model

history = model.fit(trainX, trainy, validation_data=(testX,
testy), epochs=100, verbose=0)

# evaluate the model

_, train_mse = model.evaluate(trainX, trainy, verbose=0)

_, test_mse = model.evaluate(testX, testy, verbose=0)

print('Train: %.3f, Test: %.3f' % (train_mse, test_mse))

# plot the loss during training

pyplot.subplot(211)

pyplot.title('Loss')

pyplot.plot(history.history['loss'], label='train')

pyplot.plot(history.history['val_loss'], label='test')

pyplot.legend()

# plot the mse during training

pyplot.subplot(212)

pyplot.title('Mean Squared Error')

pyplot.plot(history.history['mean_squared_error'],
label='train')

pyplot.plot(history.history['val_mean_squared_error'],
label='test')

pyplot.legend()
```

**pyplot.show()**

When the model is executed, it will return the mean square error for both the train and the test datasets. Again, due to the stochastic nature of the algorithm, the results may differ; hence you should execute the model for a number of times. The model has learned the problem to achieve an error that is almost zero:

**Train: 0.002, Test: 0.002**

The generated line plot shows that the MAE converges but it shows a bumpy course, but the MSE dynamics are not affected greatly. Our target variable is a standard Gaussian without large outliers, meaning that MAE will not be a good fit in this case.

## Binary Classification Loss Functions

Binary classification refers to the predictive modeling problems in which examples are assigned one of two labels.

Problems in this case are framed as predicting whether a value is a 0 or 1, and we implement it as predicting the probability of a value belongs to the class value 1. We will be discussing the loss functions that are appropriate for the binary classification predictive modeling problems. Examples will be generated from circles test problem of the scikit-learn library. 1000 samples will be generated and a statistical noise of 10% will be added.

**# generate the circles**

**X, y = make_circles(n_samples=1000, noise=0.1, random_state=1)**

A scatterplot of the dataset can be created to obtain an idea of the problem that we are modeling. Here is the complete example:

**# a scatterplot of circles dataset with the points being colored by class**

**from sklearn.datasets import make_circles**

```python
from matplotlib import pyplot

from numpy import where

# generate the circles

X, y = make_circles(n_samples=1000, noise=0.1,
random_state=1)

# select the indices of the points with each class label

for i in range(2):

                    samples_ix = where(y == i)

                    pyplot.scatter(X[samples_ix, 0],
X[samples_ix, 1], label=str(i))

pyplot.legend()

pyplot.show()
```

A scatter plot of the examples will be generated after execution of the above code.

We can now split the dataset into train and test sets:

```python
# split the dataset into train and test sets

n_train = 500

trainX, testX = X[:n_train, :], X[n_train:, :]

trainy, testy = y[:n_train], y[n_train:]
```

Let us create a simple MLP to address the problem:

```python
# define the model

model = Sequential()
```

```
model.add(Dense(50, input_dim=2, activation='relu',
kernel_initializer='he_uniform'))
```

```
model.add(Dense(1, activation='...'))
```

We will use stochastic descent gradient to fit the model and use a default learning rate of 0.01 and a momentum of 0.9:

```
opt = SGD(lr=0.01, momentum=0.9)
```

```
model.compile(loss='...', optimizer=opt, metrics=['accuracy'])
```

The model will be run for 200 epochs then we will evaluate it against loss and accuracy at the end of every epoch for the purpose of plotting the learning curves:

**# fit the model**

```
history = model.fit(trainX, trainy, validation_data=(testX,
testy), epochs=200, verbose=0)
```

The basis for the problem has been obtained. Let us explore how to use loss functions on it.

**Binary Cross-Entropy Loss**

Cross-entropy forms the default loss function for use in binary classification problems. It should be used in classification problems where the target values belong to the set {0,1}.

To use cross-entropy in Keras library, we can specify the binary_crossentropy parameter during the time of compiling the model as shown below:

```
model.compile(loss='binary_crossentropy', optimizer=opt,
metrics=['accuracy'])
```
With this function, the output layer should be configured with only a single layer then we use a sigmoid activation function for the purpose of predicting the probability of class 1.

```
model.add(Dense(1, activation='sigmoid'))
```

Here is the complete example showing how to use MLP with cross-entropy loss for two circles binary classification problem:

```
# mlp for circles problem with a cross entropy loss

from sklearn.datasets import make_circles

from keras.layers import Dense

from keras.models import Sequential

from matplotlib import pyplot

from keras.optimizers import SGD

# generate a 2d classification dataset

X, y = make_circles(n_samples=1000, noise=0.1,
random_state=1)

# split the dataset into train and test sets

n_train = 500

trainX, testX = X[:n_train, :], X[n_train:, :]

trainy, testy = y[:n_train], y[n_train:]

# define the model

model = Sequential()

model.add(Dense(50, input_dim=2, activation='relu',
kernel_initializer='he_uniform'))

model.add(Dense(1, activation='sigmoid'))

opt = SGD(lr=0.01, momentum=0.9)

model.compile(loss='binary_crossentropy', optimizer=opt,
metrics=['accuracy'])
```

```
# fit the model

history = model.fit(trainX, trainy, validation_data=(testX,
testy), epochs=200, verbose=0)

# evaluate model

_, train_acc = model.evaluate(trainX, trainy, verbose=0)

_, test_acc = model.evaluate(testX, testy, verbose=0)

print('Train: %.3f, Test: %.3f' % (train_acc, test_acc))

# plot the loss during training

pyplot.subplot(211)

pyplot.title('Loss')

pyplot.plot(history.history['loss'], label='train')

pyplot.plot(history.history['val_loss'], label='test')

pyplot.legend()

# plot the accuracy during training

pyplot.subplot(212)

pyplot.title('Accuracy')

pyplot.plot(history.history['acc'], label='train')

pyplot.plot(history.history['val_acc'], label='test')

pyplot.legend()

pyplot.show()
```

The model returns the classification accuracy for both the train and test sets when executed:

**Train: 0.836, Test: 0.852**

The above shows that the model was able to attain an accuracy of 83% on the train set and an accuracy of 85% on the test set. This shows that our model is neither over nor under fit.

**Hinge Loss**

This is an alternative to the cross-entropy when it comes to binary classification problems. It was developed to be used for Support Vector Machines (SVM).

This loss function should be used for binary classification problems in which the target values belong to the set {-1,1}. We should first modify the variable to have these values in the set:

**# change the y from {0,1} to {-1,1}**

**y[where(y == 0)] = -1**

To use the hinge loss function, we need to specify the parameter *hinge* during the compile time of the model:

**model.compile(loss='hinge', optimizer=opt, metrics=['accuracy'])**

The output layer of the model should be configured to have a single node and use the hyperbolic tangent activation function as it can output a single value that is within the range of [-1,1].

**model.add(Dense(1, activation='tanh'))**

The complete MLP code should be as follows:

**# mlp for circles problem with a hinge loss**

**from sklearn.datasets import make_circles**

**from keras.layers import Dense**

**from keras.models import Sequential**

```
from keras.optimizers import SGD

from numpy import where

from matplotlib import pyplot


# generate a 2d classification dataset

X, y = make_circles(n_samples=1000, noise=0.1,
random_state=1)

# change the y from {0,1} to {-1,1}

y[where(y == 0)] = -1

# split the dataset into train and test sets

n_train = 500

trainX, testX = X[:n_train, :], X[n_train:, :]

trainy, testy = y[:n_train], y[n_train:]

# define the model

model = Sequential()

model.add(Dense(50, input_dim=2, activation='relu',
kernel_initializer='he_uniform'))

model.add(Dense(1, activation='tanh'))

opt = SGD(lr=0.01, momentum=0.9)

model.compile(loss='hinge', optimizer=opt,
metrics=['accuracy'])

# fit the model
```

```python
history = model.fit(trainX, trainy, validation_data=(testX,
testy), epochs=200, verbose=0)

# evaluate the model

_, train_acc = model.evaluate(trainX, trainy, verbose=0)

_, test_acc = model.evaluate(testX, testy, verbose=0)

print('Train: %.3f, Test: %.3f' % (train_acc, test_acc))

# plot the loss during training

pyplot.subplot(211)

pyplot.title('Loss')

pyplot.plot(history.history['loss'], label='train')

pyplot.plot(history.history['val_loss'], label='test')

pyplot.legend()

# plot the accuracy during training

pyplot.subplot(212)

pyplot.title('Accuracy')

pyplot.plot(history.history['acc'], label='train')

pyplot.plot(history.history['val_acc'], label='test')

pyplot.legend()

pyplot.show()
```

The model will return the classification accuracy of the model on
both the test and train sets. Since the algorithm is stochastic, the
results may differ, hence you should consider executing the model
for a number of times.

The model is less accurate compared to when using the cross-entropy, with the accuracy on both the training and test sets being less than 80%:

**Train: 0.792, Test: 0.740**

**Squared Hinge Loss**

The following code shows how we can apply this loss function:

```
# mlp for circles problem with a squared hinge loss

from sklearn.datasets import make_circles

from keras.layers import Dense

from keras.models import Sequential

from matplotlib import pyplot

from keras.optimizers import SGD

from numpy import where

# generate a 2d classification dataset

X, y = make_circles(n_samples=1000, noise=0.1, random_state=1)

# change the y from {0,1} to {-1,1}

y[where(y == 0)] = -1

# split the dataset into train and test sets

n_train = 500

trainX, testX = X[:n_train, :], X[n_train:, :]

trainy, testy = y[:n_train], y[n_train:]
```

```
# define the model

model = Sequential()

model.add(Dense(50, input_dim=2, activation='relu',
kernel_initializer='he_uniform'))

model.add(Dense(1, activation='tanh'))

opt = SGD(lr=0.01, momentum=0.9)

model.compile(loss='squared_hinge', optimizer=opt,
metrics=['accuracy'])

# fit the model

history = model.fit(trainX, trainy, validation_data=(testX,
testy), epochs=200, verbose=0)

# evaluate the model

_, train_acc = model.evaluate(trainX, trainy, verbose=0)

_, test_acc = model.evaluate(testX, testy, verbose=0)

print('Train: %.3f, Test: %.3f' % (train_acc, test_acc))

# plot the loss during training

pyplot.subplot(211)

pyplot.title('Loss')

pyplot.plot(history.history['loss'], label='train')

pyplot.plot(history.history['val_loss'], label='test')

pyplot.legend()

# plot the accuracy during training
```

pyplot.subplot(212)

pyplot.title('Accuracy')

pyplot.plot(history.history['acc'], label='train')

pyplot.plot(history.history['val_acc'], label='test')

pyplot.legend()

pyplot.show()

The model returns an accuracy that is below 70% on both the train and test sets as shown below:

**Train: 0.682, Test: 0.646**

## Metrics

With keras, you can list the metrics that you need to monitor when training your model. This can be done using the *metrics* argument then passing to it a list of function names to *compile()* method on the model. Here is an example:

**model.compile(..., metrics=['mse'])**

The metrics that you list in this case can be names of the various Keras functions or string aliases of the functions.

The values of the metrics are recorded at the end of every epoch on the training dataset. If the validation dataset is provided, then the recorded metric will also be calculated for the validation dataset.

The metrics are reported in a verbose form in the history object which is returned after calling the *fit()* function. The metric function name is normally used as the key of the metric values. For metrics of validation dataset, we should use the *val_* prefix to the key.

## Keras Regression Metrics

The following is a list of keras metrics that can be used for regression problems:

- Mean Squared Error - the mean_squared_error, MSE or mse.
- Mean Absolute Error - the mean_absolute_error, MAE, mae.
- Mean Absolute Percentage Error - the mean_absolute_percentage_error, MAPE, mape.
- Cosine Proximity- the cosine_proximity, cosine.

These can be tracked on a regression problem as demonstrated in the following code:

```
from keras.models import Sequential

from numpy import array

from matplotlib import pyplot

from keras.layers import Dense


# prepare a sequence

X = array([0.1, 0.2, 0.3, 0.4, 0.5, 0.6, 0.7, 0.8, 0.9, 1.0])

# create a model

model = Sequential()

model.add(Dense(2, input_dim=1))

model.add(Dense(1))

model.compile(loss='mse', optimizer='adam', metrics=['mse', 'mae', 'mape', 'cosine'])

# train the model
```

```
history = model.fit(X, X, epochs=500, batch_size=len(X),
verbose=2)
```

# plot the metrics

```
pyplot.plot(history.history['mean_squared_error'])

pyplot.plot(history.history['mean_absolute_error'])

pyplot.plot(history.history['mean_absolute_percentage_error'
])

pyplot.plot(history.history['cosine_proximity'])

pyplot.show()
```

The code should return the values of the metrics for every epoch.

Note that we specified by use of the string alias names and they were referenced as the key values on history object by use of their expanded function name.

The metrics could have been specified by use of their expanded function names as shown below:

```
model.compile(loss='mse', optimizer='adam',
metrics=['mean_squared_error', 'mean_absolute_error',
'mean_absolute_percentage_error', 'cosine_proximity'])
```

The function names can also be directly specified if they have been imported into the script:

```
from keras import metrics

model.compile(loss='mse', optimizer='adam',
metrics=[metrics.mean_squared_error,
metrics.mean_absolute_error,
metrics.mean_absolute_percentage_error,
metrics.cosine_proximity])
```

The loss functions can also be used as metrics. For example, to use the Mean squared Logarithmic Error loss function as a metric, you can do the following:

**model.compile(loss='mse', optimizer='adam', metrics=['msle'])**

**Keras Classification Metrics**

Below are the Keras metrics that can be used on classification problems:

- Binary Accuracy - binary_accuracy, acc
- Categorical Accuracy - categorical_accuracy, acc
- Sparse Categorical Accuracy - sparse_categorical_accuracy
- Top k Categorical Accuracy - top_k_categorical_accuracy. You should specify a k parameter.
- Sparse Top k Categorical Accuracy - sparse_top_k_categorical_accuracy. You should specify a K parameter.

Accuracy is a special metric. The "acc" metric can be specified to report on accuracy regardless of the type of problem in question. The code given below demonstrates a binary classification problem and the use of the built-in accuracy problem:

**from numpy import array**

**from keras.layers import Dense**

**from keras.models import Sequential**

**from matplotlib import pyplot**

**# prepare a sequence**

**X = array([0.1, 0.2, 0.3, 0.4, 0.5, 0.6, 0.7, 0.8, 0.9, 1.0])**

**y = array([0, 0, 0, 0, 0, 1, 1, 1, 1, 1])**

```python
# create a model

model = Sequential()

model.add(Dense(2, input_dim=1))

model.add(Dense(1, activation='sigmoid'))

model.compile(loss='binary_crossentropy',
optimizer='adam', metrics=['acc'])

# train the model

history = model.fit(X, y, epochs=400, batch_size=len(X),
verbose=2)

# plot the metrics

pyplot.plot(history.history['acc'])

pyplot.show()
```

When the model is executed, it will report the accuracy metric at the end of every training epoch.

## Custom Metrics

Keras allows us to specify our own metrics and specify the name of the function in the list of functions for the "metrics" argument when calling the *compile()* method on the model.

If you examine the code for any metric, you can get an idea about how to create your own custom metric. For example, here is the code for the mean_square_error loss function metric in Keras:

```python
def mean_squared_error(y_true, y_pred):

    return K.mean(K.square(y_pred - y_true), axis=-1)
```

The K denotes the backend that is used by keras.

One can use the standard math functions to calculate the metrics that they are interested in the following example shows how to create a custom metric to calculate RMSE:

**from keras import backend**

**def rmse(y_true, y_pred):**

    **return backend.sqrt(backend.mean(backend.square(y_pred - y_true), axis=-1))**

The code shows that it is similar to what we have for MSE, but we have an addition of the *sqrt()* function to wrap the result.

We can try to use it in a regression example and see how it works:

**from numpy import array**

**from keras import backend**

**from keras.layers import Dense**

**from keras.models import Sequential**

**from matplotlib import pyplot**

**def rmse(y_true, y_pred):**

    **return backend.sqrt(backend.mean(backend.square(y_pred - y_true), axis=-1))**

**# prepare a sequence**

**X = array([0.1, 0.2, 0.3, 0.4, 0.5, 0.6, 0.7, 0.8, 0.9, 1.0])**

**# create a model**

```python
model = Sequential()

model.add(Dense(2, input_dim=1, activation='relu'))

model.add(Dense(1))

model.compile(loss='mse', optimizer='adam', metrics=[rmse])

# train the model

history = model.fit(X, X, epochs=500, batch_size=len(X),
verbose=2)

# plot the metrics

pyplot.plot(history.history['rmse'])

pyplot.show()
```

# 2

## Basic Classification Tasks with Keras

With the Keras, you can quickly create and train your deep learning models. Let us learn how to use keras for classification problems.

### Binary Classification

Keras can be used for performing binary classification tasks. This is what we shall be discussing in this section.

We will be using the Sonar Dataset which can be accessed from the following URL:

**https://archive.ics.uci.edu/ml/datasets/Connectionist+Bench+(Sonar,+Mines+vs.+Rocks)**

The dataset shows sonar chirp returns bouncing off different services. It has a total of 60 input variables. The purpose of this binary classification problem is to help in differentiating rocks from metal cylinders. Just download the dataset from the above URL and save it in your working directory with the name *sonar.csv*.

There are continuous variables ranging between 0 and 1. We have two output strings, M for mine and R for rock which we should convert to the integers 1 and 0.

We should begin by creating a baseline model and a result for the problem. First, let's import all the functions and classes that we will need:

**import numpy**

**import pandas**

**from keras.layers import Dense**

**from keras.models import Sequential**

**from keras.wrappers.scikit_learn import KerasClassifier**

from sklearn.preprocessing import LabelEncoder

from sklearn.model_selection import cross_val_score

from sklearn.model_selection import StratifiedKFold

from sklearn.pipeline import Pipeline

from sklearn.preprocessing import StandardScaler

We can now initialize a random number generator that will help in ensuring that we only get similar results after executing the code. This will help us during the time of debugging:

# fix a random seed for reproducibility

seed = 7

numpy.random.seed(seed)

We can now use the Pandas library to load the dataset then we split it into 60 input variables (X) and a one output variable (Y). But why have we used pandas? It is because it is good at handling strings (our output variable). It would be difficult for us to load the dataset directly using Numpy.

# load the dataset

dataframe = pandas.read_csv("sonar.csv", header=None)

dataset = dataframe.values

# split the dataset into input (X) and output (Y) variables

X = dataset[:,0:60].astype(float)

Y = dataset[:,60]

The output variable is composed of string variables. This means that they should be converted into integer values of 1 and 0.

The Scikit-learn library provides us with the LabelEncoder class that we can use for this purpose. The class works by modeling the encoding that is required by use of the whole dataset through the *fit()* function. Next, it applies encoding to create a new output variable via the *transform()* function:

**# encode the class values as integers**

**encoder = LabelEncoder()**

**encoder.fit(Y)**

**encoded_Y = encoder.transform(Y)**

After the above, we are ready to create neural network model by use of the Keras library.

We will use the scikit-learn library to evaluate our model via the stratified k-fold cross validation. This is the resampling technique that will offer you with an estimate of your model performance. It splits the data into k-parts, trains the model on all the parts other than one which is used as the test set to evaluate the performance of the model. This process will be repeated for an average k number of times and the average score obtained from all the constructed models will be used as the robust estimate of the model performance. It is stratified, which means that it will observe the output values then try to balance the number of instances belonging to every class in k-splits of the data. For us to use the Keras models with the scikit-learn library, we should use the KerasClassifier wrapper. The class takes a function to be used for creating and returning a neural network model. It takes arguments to be passed when calling the *fit()* method such as the batch size and the number of epochs.

We will begin by defining the method to create our baseline model. The model will made up of one fully connected hidden layer having similar number of neurons as the input variables. This is a great starting point when you need to create neural networks. The initialization of the weights will be done by use of a small Gaussian random number. We will also use the Rectifier activation function.

The output layer will have a single neuron for the purpose of making predictions. The sigmoid activation function will be used in this layer for the purpose of generating a probability output ranging between 0 and 1 so that it can be converted easily and automatically into crisp class values. Finally, during the training, we will use the logarithmic loss function (binary_crossentropy). It is the preferred loss function for use in binary classification problems. The model will also use the efficient Adam optimization algorithm for the gradient descent and accuracy metrics will be tracked during the training of the model:

```
# the baseline model

def create_baseline():

    # create the model

    model = Sequential()

    model.add(Dense(60, input_dim=60,
kernel_initializer='normal', activation='relu'))

    model.add(Dense(1, kernel_initializer='normal',
activation='sigmoid'))

    # Compile the model

    model.compile(loss='binary_crossentropy',
optimizer='adam', metrics=['accuracy'])

    return model
```

We should now use stratified cross validation provided by the scikit-learn model to evaluate the model. We should pass the number of the training epochs to our KerasClassifier, and we will again use some default values. We will turn off the verbose output since the model will be created for 10 times for 10-fold cross validation that will be performed:

```
# evaluate the model with a standardized dataset
```

```
estimator = KerasClassifier(build_fn=create_baseline,
epochs=100, batch_size=5, verbose=0)

kfold = StratifiedKFold(n_splits=10, shuffle=True,
random_state=seed)

results = cross_val_score(estimator, X, encoded_Y, cv=kfold)

print("Results: %.2f%% (%.2f%%)" % (results.mean()*100,
results.std()*100))
```

When the code is executed, it will return the mean and the standard deviation of estimated accuracy of our model on the unseen data:

**Baseline: 81.68% (7.26%)**

We have managed to get a very excellent score without much hard work.

We now need to rerun our model with data preparation. It is always good for us to prepare our data before we can go modeling.

We will use the Scikit-learn Pipeline. This is a wrapper that runs one or more models within a pass of a cross-validation procedure. We can use the StandardScaler then the neural network model:

```
# evaluate the baseline model with a standardized dataset

numpy.random.seed(seed)

estimators = []

estimators.append(('standardize', StandardScaler()))

estimators.append(('mlp',
KerasClassifier(build_fn=create_baseline, epochs=100,
batch_size=5, verbose=0)))

pipeline = Pipeline(estimators)
```

```python
kfold = StratifiedKFold(n_splits=10, shuffle=True,
random_state=seed)

results = cross_val_score(pipeline, X, encoded_Y, cv=kfold)

print("Standardized: %.2f%% (%.2f%%)" %
(results.mean()*100, results.std()*100))
```

The code will return a rise in the mean as shown below:

**Standardized: 84.56% (5.74%)**

There is a possibility that we have used many input variables for the problem, which has led to redundancy. We now need to run the baseline but reduce the number of neurons in the hidden layer from 60 to 30. During training, this will pile pressure on the network to choose the most important structure in input data to model.

The data will also be standardized in our previous experiment then attempt to take advantage of s small rise in performance:

```python
# a smaller model

def create_smaller():

    # create the model

    model = Sequential()

    model.add(Dense(30, input_dim=60,
kernel_initializer='normal', activation='relu'))

    model.add(Dense(1, kernel_initializer='normal',
activation='sigmoid'))

    # Compile the model

    model.compile(loss='binary_crossentropy',
optimizer='adam', metrics=['accuracy'])

    return model
```

```
estimators = []

estimators.append(('standardize', StandardScaler()))

estimators.append(('mlp',
KerasClassifier(build_fn=create_smaller, epochs=100,
batch_size=5, verbose=0)))

pipeline = Pipeline(estimators)

kfold = StratifiedKFold(n_splits=10, shuffle=True,
random_state=seed)

results = cross_val_score(pipeline, X, encoded_Y, cv=kfold)

print("Smaller: %.2f%% (%.2f%%)" % (results.mean()*100,
results.std()*100))
```

When executed, the code will return the following:

**Smaller: 86.04% (4.00%)**

The output shows that the mean estimated accuracy has received a slight boost. The standard deviation for the accuracy scores of our model has also reduced slightly.

When we create and use a neural network with many layers, we give the network the ability to collect many features then combine them to get useful nonlinear ways.

We want to check whether adding some layers to the network will make the network improve by tweaking the function that we used to create the network.

We will add another hidden layer with a total of 30 neurons. This will come after our first hidden layer. Our network topology is now as follows:

**60 inputs -> [60 -> 30] -> 1 output**

With this, the network will be given an opportunity to model all the input variables before it is bottlenecked and made to halve the representational capacity, which also what we did with our smaller network.

We don't have to squeeze the representation of our inputs, but we will add another hidden layer to aid the process:

```python
# a larger model

def create_larger():

    # create the model

    model = Sequential()

    model.add(Dense(60, input_dim=60, kernel_initializer='normal', activation='relu'))

    model.add(Dense(30, kernel_initializer='normal', activation='relu'))

    model.add(Dense(1, kernel_initializer='normal', activation='sigmoid'))

    # Compile the model

    model.compile(loss='binary_crossentropy', optimizer='adam', metrics=['accuracy'])

    return model

estimators = []

estimators.append(('standardize', StandardScaler()))

estimators.append(('mlp', KerasClassifier(build_fn=create_larger, epochs=100, batch_size=5, verbose=0)))

pipeline = Pipeline(estimators)
```

```
kfold = StratifiedKFold(n_splits=10, shuffle=True,
random_state=seed)

results = cross_val_score(pipeline, X, encoded_Y, cv=kfold)

print("Larger: %.2f%% (%.2f%%)" % (results.mean()*100,
results.std()*100))
```

The model returns the following results:

**Larger: 83.14% (4.52%)**

It is very clear no rise was recorded in the performance of our model. The cause of this can be a statistical noise or an indication that we need to do a further training.

# 3

## Keras for Image Classification

The way a machine perceives an image is different from the way we do. Machines only see numbers in an image. Each pixel of the image is assigned a value ranging between 0 and 255. This means that for the machine to be able to classify the image, it has to do some pre-processing in order to find patterns or features distinguishing the image from the others.

The following are the features rely on to be able to identify patterns in an image:

- Convolution - the convolution is done on an image to identify particular features in the image. Convolution will help in blurring, edge detection, sharpening, noise reduction and much on an image that can help the machine to extract specific characteristics from the image.
- Pooling - A convoluted image may be large, hence the need to reduce it. Pooling is done for the purpose of reducing an image without losing its patterns or features.
- Flattening - Flattening will transform a two-dimensional matrix of features to return a vector of features which we can feed into a classifier or a neural network.
- Full-Connection - Full connection is the process of feeding a flattened image into the neural network.

We will use Keras and TensorFlow to build our convolutional neural network model.

Consider a classification problem in which your task is to classify images into two categories, oranges or mangoes, cats or dogs etc. The images are stored in directories and the directory names are used as the labels. A set of images should be used for training and the remaining set be used for testing.

Let us begin by importing the libraries that we will require:

**from keras.models import Sequential**

from keras.layers import MaxPooling2D

from keras.layers import Convolution2D

from keras.layers import Dense

from keras.layers import Flatten

Let us now initialize our network model via the Sequential class provided by Keras:

**model = Sequential()**

Let us now create the convolutional layer:

**model.add(Convolution2D(filters = 32, kernel_size = (3, 3),**

**input_shape = (64, 64, 3),**

**activation = 'relu'))**

Let us create the pooling layer:

**model.add(MaxPooling2D(pool_size = (2, 2)))**

The *pool_size* denotes the shape of our pooling window. Let us add a second layer:

**model.add(Convolution2D(32, 3, 3, activation = 'relu'))**

**model.add(MaxPooling2D(pool_size = (2, 2)))**

Next, we create the flattening layer:

**model.add(Flatten())**

We now need to make a full connection of our network. Let us create the hidden layer:

```python
model.add(Dense(units = 128, activation = 'relu'))
```

Next, we create the output layer:

```python
model.add(Dense(units = 1, activation = 'sigmoid'))
```

We can now compile our convolutional neural network:

```python
model.compile(optimiser = 'adam', loss = 'binary_crossentropy', metrics = ['accuracy'])
```

We can now generate the image data. First, add the following import statement

```python
from keras.preprocessing.image import ImageDataGenerator
```

Then you add the following code:

```python
train_datagen = ImageDataGenerator(rescale = 1./255,

            shear_range = 0.1,

            zoom_range = 0.2,

            horizontal_flip = True)

test_datagen = ImageDataGenerator(rescale = 1./255)
```

It is now time for us to fit the images into our convolutional neural network. We will create a function that will allow the identifier to directly identify the labels from the directory names in which the image is lying. This is shown below:

```python
training_set = train_datagen.flow_from_directory('dataset/training_set',
```

```
target_size = (64, 64),


batch_size = 32,


class_mode = 'binary')

   test_set =
test_datagen.flow_from_directory('dataset/test_set',


target_size = (64, 64),


batch_size = 32,


class_mode = 'binary')
```

It is now time for us to train and evaluate the model. This can be done as follows:

```
model.fit_generator(training_set,

        samples_per_epoch = 2000,

        nb_epoch = 15,

        validation_data = test_set,

        nb_val_samples = 200)
```

The neural network model will be trained using the training set and then evaluated or tested by use of the test set.

# 4

## Keras for Text Classification

We can use recurrent neural networks to analyse sequences of text then assign labels to them. A recurrent neural network refers to the kind of neural network in which the connections made between the nodes form a directed graph in a sequence. With such a structure, it is possible for it to exhibit a dynamic temporal behaviour in a time sequence.

We will be using a recurrent neural network to train a classifier that will be used for text classification. The use of knowledge from an external embedding can help in enhancing the precision of a recurrent neural network since it will integrate new information about the words (both semantic and lexical), which is information that has readily been trained and distilled from a large corpus of data.

We will use GloVe as the pre-trained embedding. You can access this from the following URL:

**https://nlp.stanford.edu/projects/glove/**

Recurrent neural networks may seem to be difficult for one to understand due to their complexity. They come with unique structure that becomes very evident when dealing with sequential data such as videos, text, time series, DNA sequences etc. They overcome the traditional forms of neural networks.

A recurrent neural network is made up of a sequence of neural network blocks linked or connected to each other to form a chain. Each passes a message to its successor.

For us to be able to use the Keras library for text data, we should first pre-process it. This can be done using the Tokenizer class of Keras. This object will take *num_words* as the argument, which denotes the maximum number of words that are kept after the tokenization depending on word frequency.

**MAX_NB_WORDS = 20000**
**tokenizer = Tokenizer (num_words=MAX_NB_WORDS)**
**tokenizer.fit_on_texts(texts)**

After fitting the tokenizer on the data, it can be used for converting the text strings into a sequence of numbers. The numbers will then be representing the position of every word in the dictionary.

Let us use the LSTM encoder to encode all our text information of last output of the recurrent neural network. It is after this that a feed forward neural network can be executed for classification purposes.

In keras, there is a good wrapper named *bidirectional* that can make your coding experience effortless:

**sequence_input =**
**Input(shape=(MAX_SEQUENCE_LENGTH,),**
**dtype='int32')**
**embedded_sequences = embedding_layer(sequence_input)**
**l_lstm = Bidirectional(LSTM(100))(embedded_sequences)**
**preds = Dense(len(macronum), activation='softmax')(l_lstm)**
**model = Model(sequence_input, preds)**
**model.compile(loss='categorical_crossentropy',optimizer='r**
**msprop', metrics=['acc'])**

We need to give another example of text classification using recurrent neural networks in Keras. We will be training a neural network to learn the lyrics style in a music genre and we generate text lines from it. Let us first create the dataset:

**python3 utils/generate_classifier_set.py**
**corpora/corpus_banda.txt banda_subset.txt**
**random_banda.txt**

The above script will create two files, the first one being a subset of the original corpus, and all lines with at least one ignored word will be ignored. The second file will have text that is generated randomly based on some rules. Due to this, the two files have a similar size in terms of the number of lines:

Here is an example:

*$ python3 generate_random_lines.py corpora/corpus_banda.txt*

*# returns:* banda_subset.txt random_banda.txt
*$ wc* banda_subset.txt random_banda.txt
 *# returns:*

*# 126665  703435 3515098* banda_subset.txt
 *# 126665  705279 3523796* random_banda.txt

Our script for training the classifier will read the two files then create the training/test examples.

It is now time for us to train the classifier. A single training example of lyrics generator will be made of a sentence, in word by word, with the goal label being a single value, and the next word will represent it in the corpus. Here are examples:

>>> sentences[0]

# returns: ['put', 'a', 'gun', 'against', 'his']

>>> next_words[0]

# returns: 'head'

>>> sentences[1]

# returns: ['a', 'gun', 'against', 'his', 'head']

>>> next_words[1]

# returns: 'pulled'

Given the input, the output from the network for one example should be the probability of each possible word. This means that if your vocabulary has a total of 5,000 different words, its output will be composed of a vector of a total of 5000 values, with probability for every word, and all should add up to 1.

We can now move to the coding part. We will begin by creating a training set reading from files with both positive and negative examples. We will pad the sentences using *pad_and_split_sentences* since they all don't have equal length. The labels *y* will also be created to concatenate 0's and 1's with correct length:

```
good_ones = process_file(sys.argv[1])
bad_ones = process_file(sys.argv[2])

x = pad_and_split_sentences(good_ones + bad_ones)
y = [1]*len(good_ones) + [0]*len(bad_ones)
```

We can now create a dictionary, and the variable *words* will become a sorted set with different and unique words in the two files:

```
print("To read files and get unique words")
words = set([PAD_WORD])
for line in x:
    words = words.union(set(line))
words = sorted(words)
print('Unique words:', len(words))

word_indices = dict((c, i) for i, c in enumerate(words))
indices_word = dict((i, c) for i, c in enumerate(words))
```

We can then shuffle and split the dataset into training and test sets. 90% of the data will form the training set and 10% the test set:

```
sentences, labels, sentences_test, labels_test = shuffle_and_split_training_set(x, y)
```

It is now time to create the model. The vectors will be passed to a bidirectional Long short-Term memory of 64 units. We will also add a dropout to help us avoid over fitting. The output will be a dense layer of 1 and a sigmoid activation function:

```
model = Sequential()
model.add(Embedding(len(words), 32))
model.add(Bidirectional(LSTM(64)))
model.add(Dropout(dropout))
model.add(Dense(1, activation='sigmoid'))
```

We can now compile our model using the *binary_crossentropy* loss and an Adam optimizer. We will use a data generator to fit the model, whereby the labels and the examples will be fed in batches rather than feeding them at once:

```
model.compile(loss='binary_crossentropy',
        optimizer="adam",
        metrics=['accuracy'])
print(model.summary())
```

```
model.fit_generator(generator(sentences, labels,
BATCH_SIZE),
```

```
steps_per_epoch=int(len(sentences)/BATCH_SIZE) + 1,
        epochs=10,
        callbacks=callbacks_list,
        validation_data=generator(sentences_test,
labels_test, BATCH_SIZE),
```

```
validation_steps=int(len(sentences_test)/BATCH_SIZE) + 1)
```

We can now call a function that will use weights of your network on test dataset. This will give us a confusion matrix, and we will get the number of the True Positives, True Negatives, False Positives, False Negatives:

```
confusion_matrix(sentences_test, labels_test, True)
```

The following command will help us to launch the training:

```
$ python3 classifier_train.py <positive_examples_file>
<negative_examples_file>
```

After training for about 10 epochs, we get a training accuracy of 98%. For the training set and an accuracy of 94.3% for the test set. This is good percentage since we have some ambiguity in the sides.

# 5

## Advanced Keras

### Callbacks

It can be difficult for one to troubleshoot deep learning models. However, this can be made much easier by use of the Keras callbacks. With Keras callbacks, one can easily fix bugs, and they are good for building of better models. With them, you can visualize the progress of your model training, and they can prevent over fitting from occurring by modifying the learning rate after each epoch or by facilitating early stopping. The Keras callbacks will return information from the training algorithm as the training continues. You must note that callbacks are simply functions. This means that you can create custom callbacks if you need.

Examples of Keras in-built callbacks include BaseLogger, History, ModelCheckpoint, CSVLogger, earlyStopping, RemoteMonitor, LearningRateScheduler etc. The following code demonstrates how you can create your own callback in Keras:

```
import keras


class My_Callback(keras.callbacks.Callback):

  def on_train_begin(self, logs={}):

    return


  def on_train_end(self, logs={}):

    return
```

```python
def on_epoch_begin(self, logs={}):

    return


def on_epoch_end(self, epoch, logs={}):

    return


def on_batch_begin(self, batch, logs={}):

    return


def on_batch_end(self, batch, logs={}):

    self.losses.append(logs.get('loss'))

    return
```

The code can be understood with much ease. We have imported the class from *keras.callbacks.Callback*, and it already has the *on {train, epoch, batch} {begin, end}* functions. Our task is only to redefine them. We can also overload them. An instance of the callback can then be put as the argument to the Keras's *model.fit* function.

## Checkpoints

Application check pointing refers to a fault tolerance technique applied in long-running processes. With check pointing, a snapshot of the system is created in preparation for uncertain events like system failure.

During the training of the deep learning models, a checkpoint denotes the weights of the model. We can use these weights for making predictions as is, or we used them as the basis for the ongoing training.

With the ModelCheckpoint callback provided by Keras, you can define where you need to checkpoint the weights of your model. You can also define the way the file will be named and the circumstances under which a checkpoint of the model will be created.

We can rely on check pointing to output the weights of a model every time that the model shows an improvement after training.

We will be creating a small dataset to operate on the Pima Indians onset of diabetes binary classification problem. The dataset file should be kept in your working directory with the name pima-indians-diabetes.csv. You can download this dataset from the following URL:

https://raw.githubusercontent.com/jbrownlee/Datasets/master/pima-indians-diabetes.data.csv

We will be using 33% of this data for validation purposes. The created checkpoint will only save the network weights when an improvement occurs in the classification accuracy on validation dataset:

**# Checkpoint the weights after an improvement in validation accuracy**

**from keras.models import Sequential**

**from keras.callbacks import ModelCheckpoint**

**from keras.layers import Dense**

**import numpy**

```python
import matplotlib.pyplot as plt


# fix a random seed for reproducibility

seed = 7

numpy.random.seed(seed)

# load the pima indians dataset

dataset = numpy.loadtxt("pima-indians-diabetes.csv",
delimiter=",")

# split dataset into input (X) and output (Y) variables

X = dataset[:,0:8]

Y = dataset[:,8]

# create a model

model = Sequential()

model.add(Dense(12, input_dim=8,
kernel_initializer='uniform', activation='relu'))

model.add(Dense(8, kernel_initializer='uniform',
activation='relu'))

model.add(Dense(1, kernel_initializer='uniform',
activation='sigmoid'))

# Compile the model
```

```
model.compile(loss='binary_crossentropy',
optimizer='adam', metrics=['accuracy'])
```

# checkpoint

```
filepath="weights-improvement-{epoch:02d}-
{val_acc:.2f}.hdf5"
```

```
checkpoint = ModelCheckpoint(filepath, monitor='val_acc',
verbose=1, save_best_only=True, mode='max')
```

```
callbacks_list = [checkpoint]
```

# Fit model

```
model.fit(X, Y, validation_split=0.33, epochs=150,
batch_size=10, callbacks=callbacks_list, verbose=0)
```

After executing the model, you will be able to see the epochs that improved and the ones that didn't. A number of files will also be generated in your working directory and these will have the network weights in HDF5 format.

We have just demonstrated a simple check pointing strategy. However, it has a weakness in that it may end up creating many check-point files in case the validation accuracy moves up and down during the training epochs. However, it is good in that you will get a snapshot of best model that was discovered during the process.

If you need to create a simple checkpoint, it will be good for you to save the weights of your model in one file, only when the validation accuracy shows an improvement. To do this, we can rely on the code given above, but we make the output filename to remain fixed. This means that we don't include the epoch or score information.

Let us now be writing the weights of the model to a file named weights.best.hdf5only when the classification accuracy of the model on our validation dataset shows an improvement over the best that has been seen so far:

```
# Checkpoint weights for the best model on the validation accuracy

from keras.models import Sequential

from keras.callbacks import ModelCheckpoint

from keras.layers import Dense

import matplotlib.pyplot like plt

import numpy

# fix a random seed for reproducibility

seed = 7

numpy.random.seed(seed)

# load the pima indians dataset

dataset = numpy.loadtxt("pima-indians-diabetes.csv", delimiter=",")

# split the dataset into input (X) and output (Y) variables

X = dataset[:,0:8]

Y = dataset[:,8]

# create a model
```

```python
model = Sequential()

model.add(Dense(12, input_dim=8,
kernel_initializer='uniform', activation='relu'))

model.add(Dense(8, kernel_initializer='uniform',
activation='relu'))

model.add(Dense(1, kernel_initializer='uniform',
activation='sigmoid'))

# Compile the model

model.compile(loss='binary_crossentropy',
optimizer='adam', metrics=['accuracy'])

# checkpoint

filepath="weights.best.hdf5"

checkpoint = ModelCheckpoint(filepath, monitor='val_acc',
verbose=1, save_best_only=True, mode='max')

callbacks_list = [checkpoint]

# Fit model

model.fit(X, Y, validation_split=0.33, epochs=150,
batch_size=10, callbacks=callbacks_list, verbose=0)
```

After running the model, you will be able to see the weight file in the local directory. This is good checkpoint that you can always use when running your experiments. Your best model will be saved so that you can use it at a later time. With this, you will not have to include your code manually in order to track and serialize your best model during training.

Now that you have known how to checkpoint your neural network models, you should learn how to load them, that is, load a check pointed deep learning model and begin to use it.

Note that the checkpoint will only include the weights of the model. It will assume that you are aware of the structure of the network. This can be serialized to a file in YAML or JSON format.

In the example given below, the structure of the model is known, and we are loading the best weights. These weights have been kept in our working directory in a file named *weights.best.hdf5*. We will then use the loaded model to make predictions on our whole dataset:

```
# Loading and using weights from a checkpoint

from keras.models import Sequential

from keras.callbacks import ModelCheckpoint

from keras.layers import Dense

import numpy

import matplotlib.pyplot like plt


# fix a random seed for reproducibility

seed = 7

numpy.random.seed(seed)

# create a model

model = Sequential()
```

```python
model.add(Dense(12, input_dim=8,
kernel_initializer='uniform', activation='relu'))

model.add(Dense(8, kernel_initializer='uniform',
activation='relu'))

model.add(Dense(1, kernel_initializer='uniform',
activation='sigmoid'))

# load the weights

model.load_weights("weights.best.hdf5")

# Compile the model (good for making predictions)

model.compile(loss='binary_crossentropy',
optimizer='adam', metrics=['accuracy'])

print("Created model and loaded weights from file")

# load the pima indians dataset

dataset = numpy.loadtxt("pima-indians-diabetes.csv",
delimiter=",")

# split into input (X) and output (Y) variables

X = dataset[:,0:8]

Y = dataset[:,8]

# estimate the accuracy on entire dataset using the loaded
weights

scores = model.evaluate(X, Y, verbose=0)
```

```
print("%s: %.2f%%" % (model.metrics_names[1],
scores[1]*100))
```

The code returns an accuracy of 77.73%.

# Final notes

This marks the end of this book. Keras is a deep learning library developed in Python programming language. It is a good library for creating, training and testing of deep learning models. Deep learning is all about neural networks, hence the Keras library was meant for development of neural network models. It is a great option for you if you need to learn how to create deep learning models in Python. It comes with numerous functions and options that make your work of training neural network models much easy. Deep learning models are good for extracting patterns and trends from huge datasets. Keras can run on top libraries such as Theano, TensorFlow and CNTK. During its development, it was meant for fast experimentation. The library was developed for human beings rather than machines, which has made it more user-friendly. It gives a high priority to user experience. The user is only expected to go through few steps before completing any particular action.

www.ingramcontent.com/pod-product-compliance
Lightning Source LLC
Chambersburg PA
CBHW071007050326
40689CB00014B/3529